FAITH AS JOURNEY

Dr. Robert A. Wierenga, D.Min., M.Div.

First Edition

Wierenga Consulting, LLC

Tampa Bay, Florida

© 2017 Robert A. Wierenga. All rights reserved.

ISBN 978-0-692-91334-5

The Scripture quotations contained herein are from the New Revised Standard Version Bible, copyright © 1989, by the Division of Christian Education of the National Council of the Churches of Christ in the U.S.A. Used by permission. All rights reserved.

TABLE OF CONTENTS

Table of Contents 1
Preface 3

PART ONE: FAITH JOURNEYS

Chapter 1 - Ruth's Faith Journey: HOME 5
Chapter 2 - Philip's Faith Journey: LISTEN 14
Chapter 3 - Rahab's Faith Journey: COURAGE 23
Chapter 4 - Elijah's Faith Journey: RESILIENCE 32
Chapter 5 - Esther's Faith Journey: COMPASSION 41
Chapter 6 - Paul's Faith Journey: CHANGE 50
Chapter 7 - Mary's Faith Journey: FAMILY 59
Chapter 8 - Nehemiah's Faith Journey: REPAIR 68
Chapter 9 - Lydia's Faith Journey: OPEN 77
Chapter 10 - Peter's Faith Journey: HOPE 86

PART TWO: LITURGIES AND POEMS

A New Song 96
And His Face Shone 97
Being a Father 99
Easter Light 100
First Palm Sunday 101
Follow Me 102
Gifts 103
In the Name of the Lord 104
Living and Revealing God 105
Make Me Wise 106
That Stone's Too Big 107
The Seventh Month 109
The World Needs Easter 110

This Easter Morning	111
Thrones and Chairs	112
Waiting Father	113
What I Have	114
When Is Christmas?	115
Where Do We Look?	116
Where?	118
Word	119

PREFACE

This book is about journeys. About twenty miles east of Jerusalem is a site on the Jordan River known as *Al-Maghtas* in Arabic. It is mentioned in English as "Bethany Beyond the Jordan" in the Gospel of John (1:28). This is the most likely place where Jesus was baptized by John the Baptist. I journeyed to this site to see the archeological dig and imagine what it was like when Jesus encountered John. The final road to this historic place is unpaved and dusty. Our group hiked in over 100°F under the August sun. The photos above show the trail map and me at the site. This journey was not easy, but was worth the effort.

The Bible is filled with accounts of journeys. In this book, we will explore ten of them: five women and five men; five in the Old Testament and five in the New. These journeys were difficult. Genuine faith in God is not essentially *doctrine* or *organization*. Living faith is nurtured by the experiences we have on our unique daily *journey*.

This book began as a series of ten messages that I shared with the congregation of Lake Seminole Presbyterian Church in Tampa Bay, Florida.

PART ONE
FAITH JOURNEYS

Chapter 1
"HOME"

RUTH'S FAITH JOURNEY
"HOME"

"Where you go, I will go;
and where you lodge, I will lodge."
(Ruth 1:16)

RUTH 1:15-19

So she said, "See, your sister-in-law has gone back to her people and to her gods; return after your sister-in-law." But Ruth said, "Do not press me to leave you or to turn back from following you! Where you go, I will go; where you lodge, I will lodge; your people shall be my people, and your God my God. Where you die, I will die—there will I be buried. May the Lord do thus and so to me, and more as well, if even death parts me from you!" When Naomi saw that she was determined to go with her, she said no more to her.

"HOME"

HOME is such a simple word ...
    only four letters
    just one syllable.
Germans call it HAUS.
It is CASA in Spanish.

Yet, simple words convey deep meanings:
    Joy, Hope, Love
    Peace and HOME.

Is HOME a building?
Some live in large, fancy structures
    of many rooms and spacious hallways.
Most call a simple building HOME
    with modest dimensions
    and an unassuming appearance.

Maybe HOME is a fairy tale.
It sounds nice, but is just an illusion.
The word generates warm feelings
but these are only daydreams.
They have no place in the real world.

But, could HOME be both ...
    the beginning of our journey
    and its destination?
HOME is where ...
    we are loved for who we are
    and for what God wants us to become.

RUTH'S FAITH JOURNEY
RUTH 1:15-19
HOME

Journeys are at the center of who we are as human beings. Each one of us faces a basic choice in life. Do I simply sit down where I am and vegetate? Or do I choose to journey ahead? Many times, our journeys are physical as we move from one place to another. When I make a journey to see my family in western Michigan, I must fly from Tampa Airport to Grand Rapids. I physically move.

There are, however, several types of journeys that we can take: emotional or intellectual. Many men and women, who were abused as children, deal with certain emotional issues as adults. During their lives, the emotional journey can be difficult. Also, for men and women in science, in the world of numbers and precise measurement, they must journey through the stages required in solving difficult problems.

This book will focus on a special human journey: our spiritual journey of faith. What role does God, does the Divine play in our life? Do we sense God's presence day-to-day? Maybe God seems distant and unknowable. We will explore "faith as journey" by walking with ten persons on their spiritual journeys. There will be five women and five men, five from the Old Testament and five from the New.

Before we begin to look at Ruth's faith journey, I would like to reflect for a moment on what faith is not. At its essence, faith is not *organization*. Now this is not saying that organization has no place in our faith experience. Many studies have shown that a healthy, an inclusive and properly functioning organization can be extremely helpful. My point is that faith, at its heart, is not a finely-tuned organization or flow chart. There is more to it.

Let me illustrate this point by looking at the description of Paul and Barnabas appointing leaders in newly-planted Christian congregations. The Book of Acts tells the story of these two men organizing followers of Jesus in cities in present-day Turkey:

> And after they had appointed elders for them in each church, with prayer and fasting they entrusted them to the Lord (Acts 14:23).

We are told *who* are the leaders of these early groups of Christians. We are not told, however, *how* they are to function as appointed leaders. As the Christian Church grew, differing styles of leadership and structure arose. While it was important to iron out how decisions were to be made, this was not the heart of the Gospel message.

Neither is *doctrine* or dogma at the heart of faith. We are very good at having arguments and fights over doctrine. For example, should Christians be baptized as infants or should they wait until they are adults? Before his ascension, Jesus tells his followers:

> "Go therefore and make disciples of all nations, baptizing them in the name of the Father and of the Son and of the Holy Spirit" (Matthew 28:19).

Well, *how* do we baptize them? *When* do we baptize them? Jesus does not answer these questions. Followers of Jesus have been arguing about these questions of doctrine for twenty centuries.

Faith is not primarily *organization*. Faith is not essentially *doctrine*. What is it? At its heart, faith is *journey*, a life-long journey.

The faith journey of Ruth helps us understand this important truth. She is the daughter-in-law of Naomi. They were living in the land of Moab and began the journey back to the land of Judah. Judah was the home of Naomi and she told Ruth not to come to a foreign land. Listen to Ruth's words as she sets out on her journey with Naomi. She feels a deep bond with Naomi and wants to make the journey to Judah with her. Ruth will not be talked out of it.

> "Do not press me to leave you or to turn back from following you. Where you go, I will go; where you lodge, I will lodge; your people shall be my people, and your God my God" (Ruth 1:16).

The journey will be from the land of Moab to the land of Judah. Moab is on the east side of the Dead Sea and Judah is on the west side.

Ruth's faith journey involves HOME. Her heart must have been torn between Moab and Judah. If she went with Naomi, would she indeed come to a "new home" in a strange land? The final stanza of our poem says,

> But could HOME be both ...
>> the beginning of our journey
>> and its destination?
>
> HOME is where ...
>> we are loved for who we are
>> and for what God wants us to become.

Something special was in store for Ruth. She would be blessed with a new home and a new family.

Faith is journey and this journey brings us to a new home. This is what Ruth's long walk from Moab to Judah teaches us. In other words, genuine faith is not static or lifeless. There is a dynamic to it. It is a response to God's call to a new home. A place where "we are loved for who we are."

REFLECTING ON RUTH'S JOURNEY

1. Some might consider Ruth to be an "immigrant" or a "refugee." Would that affect your view of her?

2. Do you agree that the essence of Faith is *Journey* and not *Doctrine* or *Organization*? Why?

3. Why is *Home* important to you?

4. How do you understand the last line of the poem: "and for what God wants us to become"?

PHILIP'S FAITH JOURNEY
"LISTEN"

Then an angel of the Lord said to Philip,
"Get up and go toward the south."
(Acts 8:26)

ACTS 8:26-31

Then an angel of the Lord said to Philip, "Get up and go toward the south to the road that goes down from Jerusalem to Gaza." (This is a wilderness road.) So he got up and went. Now there was an Ethiopian eunuch, a court official of the Candace, queen of the Ethiopians, in charge of her entire treasury. He had come to Jerusalem to worship and was returning home; seated in his chariot, he was reading the prophet Isaiah. Then the Spirit said to Philip, "Go over to this chariot and join it." So Philip ran up to it and heard him reading the prophet Isaiah. He asked, "Do you understand what you are reading?" He replied, "How can I, unless someone guides me?" And he invited Philip to get in and sit beside him.

"A STILL, SMALL VOICE"

The sound of thunder gets our attention.
Its loud clap interrupts us as
.... babies begin to cry
.... and pets hide in the corner.

The crash of a huge wave startles us.
We are face-to-face with the ocean's power.
The sea is stronger than any dam
or dike that we can build.

The roar of a jet engine overwhelms us
.... it stops our conversation
.... and limits our hearing.
Everything pauses until the plane is gone.

Sometimes God speaks with a mighty voice.
The divine Word created the heavens and the earth.
His revelation at Mt. Sinai frightened the people.
The words of Jesus raised Lazarus from the tomb.

For most of us, however, God speaks in a still, small voice.
Like Elijah, we strain to hear what seems like a whisper.
These gentle words require a calm soul.
Only attentive ears can discern God's message.

("a still, small voice" is referred to in 1 Kings 19:12)

PHILIP'S FAITH JOURNEY
ACTS 8:26-31
"LISTEN"

How is your hearing? I am writing this chapter in my home office and Molly, our Golden Retriever, is lying down not far from me. I am not concerned about missing anyone who would come to the front door of my house. Molly lets me know if the mail carrier or UPS driver brings a package. She also makes sure that I know if a neighbor is coming over for a visit. Her hearing is so much better than mine. Part of her job is listening for persons approaching our house.

How is your hearing? Are you a good listener? These questions bring us to one of the themes of Philip's faith journey. At the core of his journey is the necessity of listening to the voice of God. Only by carefully listening will he be able to travel south from Jerusalem to his destination in Gaza.

In the Bible, God speaks in both a loud voice and a small voice. The preceding poem notes this:

> For most of us, however, God speaks in a still,
>   small voice.
> Like Elijah, we strain to hear what seems like
>   a whisper.
> These gentle words require a calm soul.
> Only attentive ears can discern God's message.

This poem is based on the prophet Elijah's experience of listening for God's voice in 1 Kings chapter 19. After waiting, he hears God speaking to him in "a sound of sheer silence" (other translations say, "a still, small voice").

Philip is the central character in our reading from the Book of Acts. He is also known as "Philip the Evangelist" (Acts 21:8). We are told that he was one of the first deacons chosen and he flees Jerusalem when fellow-deacon Stephen is martyred. In our reading, Philip listens to two separate calls from God. Each of these calls teaches us about the nature of God's message along our personal journey of faith.

God's first message to Philip is a general one that gets him walking on his journey south to Gaza. We read,

> Then an angel of the Lord said to Philip, "Get up and go toward the south to the road that goes down from Jerusalem to Gaza" (Acts 8:26).

It's important to note that God's summons to journey begins in only a general way. Only later does God become more specific. It seems that Philip lives north of Jerusalem. God tells him to travel south on the road to Gaza. No more details or instructions are given. It is indeed rather general and vague. What was going on in Philip's mind? Would he begin this journey with only the most basic of information?

What about us? Are we hesitant about our faith journey because God has not revealed all of the details? This is common for us as humans. Have you ever purchased a house or rented an apartment or condo? This always involves stepping out on faith. Will the area be flooded in a storm? Will the street be torn up and repaved? A couple of blocks from Lake Seminole Presbyterian Church, a new shopping complex was recently built. For months, the people living in that area had to deal with lane closings and daily noise. The local residents could not have foreseen this chaos when they made the decision to move into this neighborhood.

We have noted that Philip receives two messages from God in our passage. The first is a general call to travel from Jerusalem south to Gaza. The purpose of this journey is not revealed. Philip must begin walking south completely by faith. Once Philip is in Gaza, he receives more specific guidance. He encounters a royal official from Ethiopia. We read in verse 29,

> Then the Spirit said to Philip, "Go over to this chariot and join it" (Acts 8:29).

God's plan for Philip's journey is that he would meet this man and clear up his confusion.

The official in the chariot is reading from the Book of Isaiah and is confused about the meaning of the passage. He appears to be reading from Isaiah chapter 53 which talks about the Suffering Servant sacrificing his life. Do the words of the prophet refer to the nation of Israel? Just who is Isaiah writing about? Is it Abraham? Is it Moses? Is it David? Listen to their conversation:

> Philip: "Do you understand what you are reading" (v. 30)?
> Official: "How can I, unless someone guides me" (v. 31)?

The door is now open for Philip to explain the meaning of Isaiah's prophetic words. He joins the official in his chariot and shows how the prophet pointed to the coming of Jesus as the long-awaited Messiah. The result is that this official believes in Jesus Christ and is baptized.

Philip's journey is successful. Its purpose is realized. This happens because he listens for God's voice. While the first divine message was vague, the next one fills in the details. What about us? Are we good listeners? We journey ahead based on what God has revealed to us. Like Philip, we trust in God's continuing guidance as we walk step-by-step.

REFLECTING ON PHILIP'S JOURNEY

1. How do you listen to God's messages? Give one example.

2. What "outside noise" distracts you from hearing what God has to say?

3. How many details do you need to know before you begin a journey?

4. Name one lesson that you have learned from the faith journey of Philip?

RAHAB'S FAITH JOURNEY
"COURAGE"

Rahab the prostitute, with her family and all who belonged to her, Joshua spared. Her family has lived in Israel ever since.
(Joshua 6:25)

JOSHUA 6:22-25

Joshua said to the two men who had spied out the land, "Go into the prostitute's house, and bring the woman out of it and all who belong to her, as you swore to her." So the young men who had been spies went in and brought Rahab out, along with her father, her mother, her brothers, and all who belonged to her—they brought all her kindred out—and set them outside the camp of Israel. They burned down the city, and everything in it; only the silver and gold, and the vessels of bronze and iron, they put into the treasury of the house of the Lord. But Rahab the prostitute, with her family and all who belonged to her, Joshua spared. Her family has lived in Israel ever since. For she hid the messengers whom Joshua sent to spy out Jericho.

"TO THE FAINT OF HEART"

There are no monuments to the faint of heart.
No one sings their praise.
There are no great deeds to write about.
Their fear and their timid nature
are not honored in the public square.

But the truly bold and courageous are few.
Most of us settle for being lukewarm followers.
We avoid the risky
and are hesitant to wander outside the box.
As the majority, we are quite content.

The faint of heart are not eager for a faith journey.
God's Spirit must first inspire them
and nudge them to take the first step.
Moses needed courage to confront an Egyptian despot.
Emboldened by God, Rahab left doomed Jericho.
Strengthened by the divine presence, Mary bore the
      Messiah.

The faint of heart are all around us
and we see one of them in the mirror.
Just as God gave courage to Moses, Rahab, and Mary,
the Almighty calls us to a journey of faith.
The faint of heart need only take one step at a time.

RAHAB'S FAITH JOURNEY
JOSHUA 6:22-25
"COURAGE"

When I hear the word, "courage," a number of persons come my mind. I think of volunteers with Doctors Without Borders, an organization that sends doctors to some of the most dangerous parts of the world to help others. I admire the courage of its volunteers who set up aid stations in the war-torn areas of Syria. Despite bombs and the shortage of medical supplies, these men and women help the wounded and comfort their families.

The name, Nelson Mandela, also captures my attention. Because of his opposition to apartheid, he was arrested and spent 27 years in a South African prison. Mandela said that he learned courage as he dealt with his jailers. Once finally released from jail, he worked for a color-blind society in South Africa. His courage inspired others. During the 1990s Nelson Mandela won the Nobel Peace Prize and was elected president at the age of 76.

Rahab's journey also teaches us about courage. We meet her in two chapters in the Book of Joshua. In chapter 2, Rahab hides two spies who were sent by Joshua to search out the city of Jericho. Because of her brave act, these spies promise that Rahab and her household will be spared when the soldiers of Israel destroy Jericho. Then in chapter 6, we see that the promise of safety is kept. When the walls of Jericho tumble down and the people of the city perish, Rabab and her household are spared.

The journey of Rahab shows us two aspects of courage. First, it takes courage to value what God has made. I am not courageous if I associate with or admire people who look like I do. I am not stretched to leave my comfort zone. I am not challenged to meet and understand persons who speak a different language and have their own customs.

One of the things that I admire about Nelson Mandela is his courage while imprisoned for 27 years. He was not afraid of the guards, if fact he befriended them and learned their language, Afrikaans. Although some of his fellow prisoners criticized him for this, Mandela had the courage to cross the divide that separated him from his jailers. In their eyes, he was inferior. It took courage to meet them as equals.

In integral part of Rahab's journey is her identity as a woman of ill repute. Listen to how the author identifies her in Joshua chapter 6:

> v. 17 "Rahab the prostitute"
> v. 22 "the prostitute's house"
> v. 25 "Rahab the prostitute"

He does not try to coverup this part of her identity. He includes it so that generations of believers will know the whole truth about Rahab of Jericho.

Rahab has value. She had the courage to hide the Israelite spies in her home. Rahab has the honor of being included in the genealogy of Jesus in Matthew 1:5. Indeed, she is someone. Her faith journey has much to teach us today.

We live, unfortunately, in a time of division and mistrust. There is a dysfunctional tribalism in many parts of the world. It takes courage for us to resist this dangerous trend and recall how Rahab the prostitute, Rahab the foreigner was honored.

Courage has another side to it. Courage enables us to journey through difficult times. One amazing aspect of Rahab's journey is that she is asked to leave her own city and go to the camp of Israel, the enemy of her friends and fellow inhabitants of Jericho. Verse 21 gives us a vivid picture of the destruction that takes place all around Rahab and her family:

> [The walls fell down] Then they devoted to destruction by the edge of the sword all in the city, both men and women, young and old, oxen, sheep, and donkeys (Joshua 6:21).

How terrifying it must have been for Rahab and her household.

In the midst of this destruction, this courageous woman led her family out of Jericho and to the camp of the enemy. That is, "enemy" in the eyes of her fellow residents. Her journey, however, has an ending filled with hope and joy. We read,

> Rahab the prostitute, with her family and all who belonged to her, Joshua spared. Her family has lived in Israel ever since. For she hid the

messengers whom Joshua sent to spy out Jericho (Joshua 6:25).

Rahab's courage, despite the violent destruction all around her, enabled her whole family to escape the sword.

Her journey from Jericho to the camp of the Israelites is truly inspiring. We can only imagine the courage it took for Rahab to lead her loved ones to an uncertain future. The previous poem expresses this well,

> Just as God gave courage to Moses, Rahab, and Mary,
> the Almighty calls us to a journey of faith.
> The faint of heart need only take one step at a time.

She had the courage to act in a dangerous time and place. Though many derided Rahab as an undesirable, as a prostitute, she is one of the most courageous characters in the Bible.

Let us ask for such courage for our own faith journey. May Rahab inspire us to continue taking one step at a time in even the most difficult of circumstances.

REFLECTING ON RAHAB'S JOURNEY

1. What inspires you about Rahab's faith journey?

2. Why did Rahab need courage to leave Jericho with her entire household?

3. If you had been in Rahab's place, what would you have felt or thought as you approached the camp of the Israelites?

4. Is it an embarrassment that Rahab's name is included in the genealogy of Jesus in the Gospel of Matthew?

ELIJAH'S FAITH JOURNEY
"RESILIENCE"

"Get up and eat, otherwise the journey will be too much for you" (1 Kings 19:7).

1 KINGS 19:4-9

But he himself went a day's journey into the wilderness, and came and sat down under a solitary broom tree. He asked that he might die: "It is enough; now, O Lord, take away my life, for I am no better than my ancestors." Then he lay down under the broom tree and fell asleep. Suddenly an angel touched him and said to him, "Get up and eat." He looked and there at his head was a cake baked on hot stones, and a jar of water. He ate and drank, and lay down again. The angel of the Lord came a second time, touched him, and said, "Get up and eat, otherwise the journey will be too much for you." He got up, and ate and drank; then he went in the strength of that food forty days and forty nights to Horeb the mount of God. At that place he came to a cave, and spent the night there.

"SKINNED KNEES"

Can you grow up without skinning your knees?
Probably not.
Moms and dads have bandaids ready for …
    Jason riding his new bike,
    Jenni climbing her favorite tree,
    and Miki running at full speed.

Skinned knees are just part of
babies becoming toddlers
toddlers becoming kids
and kids becoming teenagers.

Even big people get skinned knees.
Some days are difficult.
Some weeks test our strength.
And some months even test our faith in God.

Growing up means
getting back up
over and over and over again.

ELIJAH'S FAITH JOURNEY
1 KINGS 19:4-9
"RESILIENCE"

The Ted Williams Museum is behind the left-field wall at Tropicana Field. This is the ball park where the Tampa Bay Rays play baseball. Every game, many fans walk into this museum to look at photos of Ted Williams and to see bats, gloves, and uniforms that he used throughout his 19 seasons playing for the Boston Red Sox.

My two brothers and I are baseball fans. Before a game, all three of us visited the Ted Williams Museum. What an experience for a true fan. Number 9 was one of the greatest hitters of all time. He was the American League batting champion six times and the last player to hit over .400. Ted's lifetime batting average was .344.

Resilience is needed if anyone is to be a successful hitter in the Major Leagues. Ted Williams pointed that out many times as he talked about the fact that good hitters would fail seven times out of ten at the plate. This rate of failure would give you a .300 batting average and probably get you a spot on the All-Star team. You had to accept the fact that you would make an out many more times than you would get a hit.

What is "resilience"? Resilient men and women have the

ability to get back up after they fall. Such persons are able to switch to Plan B, if Plan A goes wrong. They continue to walk ahead step-by-step whether the sun is shining or it is raining or snowing outside.

Resilient persons are able to handle disappointment. They are not overwhelmed by setbacks. This is true of the prophet Elijah. His faith journey begins with a sense of crippling disappointment. The Book of First Kings, chapter 18 describes a contest between Elijah and 450 prophets of Baal on Mount Carmel. This prophet of the true, living God faces off against a multitude who served a false god. When Elijah's offering is consumed by fire, the people affirmed their faith in the living God of Abraham, Sarah, Isaac, and Rebekah.

This apparent victory for Elijah, however, quickly turns into a life-threatening event for the prophet. Queen Jezebel reacts by promising to hunt down and kill him. She sends a messenger to Elijah with these threatening words,

> "So may the gods do to me, and more also, if I do not make your life like the life of one of them by this time tomorrow" (1 Kings 19:2).

We are told that Elijah is now afraid for his life and hides himself in the wilderness. This disappointing turn of events has filled him with fear and despair.

What was going through Elijah's mind at this moment? He had done the right thing when he challenged the 450 prophets of Baal. It had been a great victory for the true God. Why did things go wrong? We can identify with this sense of disappointment. Too often, our faith journeys have rough patches, have difficult stretches. We wonder why God allows this to happen when nonbelievers seem to have so little trouble. In these moments of despair, it is good to remember the experience of Elijah. We should not be surprised when we encounter a rough spot on our faith journey.

How does Elijah handle this difficulty? How do we handle it? When we look again at the prophet's faith journey, we notice a key teaching: a resilient person must defy gravity.

Elijah has a hard time with the force of gravity. In our passage, we read that twice he lies down under a broom tree in the desert: verses 5 and 6. For some reason, he cannot muster the ability to overcome the pull of gravity and stand on his feet and begin his journey to Mount Horeb. Is he lazy? Does he lack faith? Is he afraid?

Resilient people of faith must overcome the temptation of inaction. In other words, they must defy gravity by getting up and walking. Inaction can be so, so tempting. We just sit around or lie around and do nothing. The closing lines of our poem, "Skinned Knees," encourage us to have a resilient faith that defies the pull of gravity:

> Some months even test our faith in God.

> Growing up means
> getting back up
> over and over and over again.

And this is what Elijah finally does. On his second attempt, he finally defies gravity and gets up.

From our reading in the Book of First Kings, we know that God will speak to him once he reaches Mount Horeb. It will be a long journey, but a fruitful one. The author gives us this description,

> He got up, and ate and drank; then he went in the strength of that food forty days and forty nights to Horeb the mount of God (1 Kings 19:8).

Without resilience, Elijah would have remained lying under the broom tree and never would have reached his journey's destination.

REFLECTING ON ELIJAH'S JOURNEY

1. Did Elijah over-react to Queen Jezebel's words?

2. Why is *resilience* so difficult to achieve?

3. Elijah felt disappointed at the beginning of the passage. Are you wrestling with some disappointments in your life?

4. How can you "defy gravity" and live as a resilient believer?

ESTHER'S FAITH JOURNEY
"COMPASSION"

"How can I bear to see the calamity
that is coming on my people?"
(Esther 8:6)

ESTHER 8:3-8

Then Esther spoke again to the king; she fell at his feet, weeping and pleading with him to avert the evil design of Haman the Agagite and the plot that he had devised against the Jews. The king held out the golden scepter to Esther, and Esther rose and stood before the king. She said, "If it pleases the king, and if I have won his favor, and if the thing seems right before the king, and I have his approval, let an order be written to revoke the letters devised by Haman son of Hammedatha the Agagite, which he wrote giving orders to destroy the Jews who are in all the provinces of the king. For how can I bear to see the calamity that is coming on my people? Or how can I bear to see the destruction of my kindred?" Then King Ahasuerus said to Queen Esther and to the Jew Mordecai, "See, I have given Esther the house of Haman, and they have hanged him on the gallows, because he plotted to lay hands on the Jews. You may write as your please with regard to the Jews, in the name of the king, and seal it with the king's ring; for an edict written in the name of the king and sealed with the king's ring cannot be revoked."

"COMPASSION"

Compassion is not neutral.
It is not an idle feeling
       or a safe emotion
       or a fleeting sensation.

Feeling a oneness with those who are
suffering, broken,
hurting, in danger;
can be risky.

Jesus felt compassion for the five thousand in Galilee
       and he fed them.
Lincoln had compassion for the enslaved in America
       and he freed them.
Mother Teresa felt compassion for the poor in Calcutta
       and she gave them shelter.

Compassion …. Risk …. Action.
It is for the warm-hearted and the bold of spirit.
The compassionate are those who
       embrace broken souls
       and walk with them on a common journey.

ESTHER'S FAITH JOURNEY
ESTHER 8:3-8
"COMPASSION"

When we look at Esther, we get an insight into the *compassion* that is needed to undertake a faith journey. We learn in the Book of Esther, chapter 2, that the family of Esther had recently been exiled to Susa in Persia when the city of Jerusalem had been captured and destroyed. She is thus part of what was known as the "Diaspora." These were the Jews who had been uprooted from their homeland and forced to journey abroad as captives or slaves.

Later in chapter 2, we learn that God's providence was guiding and protecting this young Jewish girl, Esther. Through a series of circumstances, she is chosen by the king to be the new queen.

I marvel at the details of Esther's faith journey in a foreign land. A core element of this dramatic journey is a deep-felt *compassion* for her endangered people. The poem that we just read puts it this way:

> Compassion … Risk … Action.
> It is for the warm-hearted and the bold of spirit.
> The compassionate are those who
> > embrace broken souls
> > and walk with them on a common journey.

These poetic lines point out that compassionate people

have *compelling* faith journeys. As they make their life pilgrimage, there is something meaningful and exciting about what is happening.

Esther's compassionate journey is certainly a compelling one. It is not an ordinary story. She is a young Jewish girl in the Persian city of Susa. She is a foreigner. Esther is also an orphan. Her life changes dramatically when the Persian Empire begins searching for a new queen. Esther is one of the many maidens presented to the king. She pleases him and is selected. What an amazing story.

Indeed, compassionate people, like Esther, have compelling journeys. Their lives are far from boring. Dean Lesnett was a member of the church I served in Tampa Bay, Florida. He was a Marine who had fought in World War II. When I conducted his funeral, I shared some of what I had learned about Dean through many conversations with him. Beneath his gruff exterior, was a man who felt genuine compassion for others. Dean told me about his upbringing in Pennsylvania before the war. Then serving as a gunner on an aircraft carrier, the USS Intrepid, he distinguished himself by fighting off kamikaze attacks.

As I listened to Dean's life-story, it was obvious that he had lived a compelling life. The formative events in his childhood took on special meaning as they helped shape his basic values. His heart-felt bond with fellow Marines in his unit and his bravery in battle made the account of his journey riveting. One could see God at work in his long life.

Compassionate people have *compelling* journeys. They also have *connected* journeys. They are not isolated from those around them. They are always nurturing old bonds and developing new ones.

When we look at the story of young Esther we note that as the new queen, she had an important choice to make. She became aware of the plot to kill her fellow exiles. Should she get involved? How tempting to just stay within the protected walls of the royal palace. Queen Esther, however, chooses a different path. She says to the king,

> "How can I bear to see the calamity that is coming on my people? Or how can I bear to see the destruction of my kindred" (Esther 8:6)?

Esther takes a step of faith and acts out of compassion for her fellow Jews. Her faith journey is *connected* to what happens to her fellow exiles. She reveals the plot to the king and thus saves her people from imminent destruction.

Esther's close ties with her people in exile, remind me of how Jesus felt connected to the people in his own day. We read in the Gospel of Matthew,

> When he [Jesus] saw the crowds, he had compassion for them, because they were harassed and helpless, like sheep without a shepherd (Matthew 9:36).

Like Esther, *compassion* was an essential element in the

journey of Jesus. This was revealed as he emotionally *connected* with those who followed him.

This element of compassion can be risky. Esther had to weigh the consequences of talking to the Persian king about the plot against her fellow Jews. Jesus eventually died on a Roman cross. This aspect of a compassionate faith journey is noted in our poem,

> Feeling a oneness with those who are
> suffering, broken,
> hurting, in danger;
> can be risky.

Just ask Esther. Just ask Jesus.

The story of Queen Esther inspires us to make sure that our faith journey is energized by *compassion*. This deep feeling of compassion will rescue our journey from being harmed by a sense of legalism or superiority. Such a compassionate journey will be both *compelling* and *connected*.

REFLECTING ON ESTHER'S JOURNEY

1. Why was *compassion* a risky part of Queen Esther's faith journey?

2. Several events made Dean Lesnet's journey a *compelling* one. Name one formative event in your life's journey.

3. Is it difficult for me to feel *connected* with certain people? Why?

4. Would Queen Esther be welcomed or despised today?

PAUL'S FAITH JOURNEY
"CHANGE"

Now as he was going along and approaching Damascus, suddenly a light from heaven flashed around him.
(Acts 9:3)

ACTS 9:1-9

Meanwhile Saul [Paul], still breathing threats and murder against the disciples of the Lord, went to the high priest and asked him for letters to the synagogues at Damascus, so that if he found any who belonged to the Way, men or women, he might bring them bound to Jerusalem. Now as he was going along and approaching Damascus, suddenly a light from heaven flashed around him. He fell to the ground and heard a voice saying to him, "Saul, Saul, why do you persecute me?" He asked, "Who are you, Lord?" The reply came, "I am Jesus, whom you are persecuting. But get up and enter the city, and you will be told what you are to do." The men who were traveling with him stood speechless because they heard the voice but saw no one. Saul got up from the ground, and though his eyes were open, he could see nothing; so they led him by the hand and brought him into Damascus. For three days he was without sight, and neither ate nor drank.

"DIGGING IN MY HEELS"

"Spring is the best season of the year.
Nothing even comes close."
I have their attention now.
How could anyone disagree with me?
"With Spring comes budding plants,
Warmer weather, and singing birds."

I hear my friends chuckle.
Some even roll their eyes as they smile.
"But what about Summer?
The days are longer,
Water is warm enough for swimming,
Time for picnics and ball games."

I dig in my heels and won't budge.
Another friend speaks up for Fall.
"Leaves turn bright red or orange or yellow.
Children play in piles of them.
The autumn sky is deep blue
And the air is crisp and pleasant."

No change for me.
My mind's made up and I'm convinced.
Then someone comes to the defense of Winter.
"The sound of crunching snow,
The sight of snow-covered trees against a clear sky,
The warmth of a fireplace as evening comes."

But my heels are still dug in ......
Why?

PAUL'S FAITH JOURNEY
ACTS 9:1-9
"CHANGE"

Is change easy to take or is it hard? It depends on the person you ask. Some of us are very comfortable with change. Just because something is *new* does not bother us or intimidate us. Not everyone, however, has this reaction to the new. Some are afraid of changes and will resist what is different.

I've made many trips to Tampa International Airport. If I'm not catching a plane, I'm either taking someone to the airport or picking someone up. In Tampa Bay, driving to the airport is an adventure. A number of heavily-travelled roads go to that part of the city. It seems like there is constant road construction so you must pay close attention to any lane changes. Again, some drivers handle these endless changes calmly while others get easily frustrated. Which group am I in? It depends on the day.

This chapter looks at the faith journey of the Apostle Paul. He is travelling north from Jerusalem to the city of Damascus. It is a journey of about 160 miles. During this journey, a fundamental change happens to Paul. The story of this change has much to teach us today.

In my ministry, I have spent much time working with the dynamics of change. The famous scientist, Sir Isaac Newton, has helped me understand the various aspects of change. It was 300 years ago that he developed his famous

Three Laws of Motion. These fundamental laws of physics are taught in schools all over the world. Our aversion to change illustrates Newton's First Law of Motion. This is also called the Law of Inertia. It states that if an object is stationary, it will remain stationary until something or someone moves it. And if an object is moving in a certain direction, it will continue moving in that direction unless another force intervenes.

Paul's journey illustrates this law of physics. He tells us that he grew up as a Pharisee. He thus had the mindset of a rigid enforcer of the Torah. It seems that Paul was an aggressive crusader in this regard. We first meet Paul in the Book of Acts when Stephen, the first Christian martyr, is stoned to death. We read,

> Then they dragged him [Stephen] out of the city and began to stone him; and the witnesses laid their coats at the feet of a young man named Saul [Paul] …. And Saul approved of their killing him" (Acts 9:58, 8:1).

It's clear that Paul's religious training had set him on a path to oppose and then persecute the followers of Jesus. He saw their interpretation of the Torah as dangerous. The High Priest in Jerusalem has given Paul letters which enable him to go to Damascus and arrest the new Christians.

Because of Paul's rigid view of Torah, he was trapped in a state of inertia. His faith journey was consumed by a fanatical desire to erase Jesus' teachings and followers from his homeland and beyond.

Does Paul's state of inertia sound familiar? If our faith journey is simply stationary or if we just refuse to make any needed changes, then we mirror Paul's unfortunate situation. The previous poem sums up our stubbornness,

> No change for me.
> My mind's made up and I'm convinced …
> My heels are still dug in

If this is our attitude toward life and faith, then how can a genuine, life-giving faith journey even be possible?

It's time to go back to Isaac Newton's First Law of Motion. This brilliant scientist noted that the only way to change inertia was to bring to bear an outside force. The only way Paul would change was if he encountered someone or something dramatic in his life.

This actually happened to Paul on his journey from Jerusalem to Damascus. We read,

> Now as he was going along and approaching Damascus, suddenly a light from heaven flashed around him. He fell to the ground and heard a voice saying to him, "Saul, Saul, why do you persecute me" (Acts 9:3-4)?

The voice identifies itself as the Risen Christ. This was the only way that Paul's narrow perspective could be changed.

God simply had to intervene while he was on his journey to Damascus.

It might be that we too are resistant to change as we walk along our journey. It is easy to give in to the temptation to be stubborn and unyielding. Like Paul, it might be that only God's intervention can open us up to new possibilities. In light of this, it's important that we do not close our ears to the divine voice. The voice of God may very well be the only thing that can get us out of our rut and embrace life-giving change.

REFLECTING ON PAUL'S JOURNEY

1. Is Paul's stubborn attitude common or uncommon today?

2. Name one time when you struggled with a major change in your life. How long did you struggle?

3. Why is change so difficult for some people?

4. What is one take-away for you from the faith journey of Paul?

MARY'S FAITH JOURNEY
"FAMILY"

In those days Mary set out and went with
haste to a Judean town in the hill country (Luke 1:39).

LUKE 1:39-45

In those days Mary set out and went with haste to a Judean town in the hill country, where she entered the house of Zachariah and greeted Elizabeth. When Elizabeth heard Mary's greeting, the child leaped in her womb. And Elizabeth was filled with the Holy Spirit and exclaimed with a loud cry, "Blessed are you among women, and blessed is the fruit of your womb. And why has this happened to me, that the mother of my Lord comes to me? For as soon as I heard the sound of your greeting, the child in my womb leaped for joy. And blessed is she who believed that there would be a fulfillment of what was spoken to her by the Lord."

"CORDS THAT BIND"

What's the glue that keeps a family connected?
When faced with stress and distractions,
are there cords that hold together
clashing egos and conflicting goals?

When a baby arrives,
the whole family smiles.
As the proud parents show off
a little boy or little girl,
a contagion of joy fills the room.
God's gift of new life
becomes a cord that unites.

Nature invites us to be explorers.
Rivers and mountains beckon
girls, boys, moms, dads, cousins
and grandparents.
Walking along a path in the woods
creates moments that are cords
binding the generations.

Then, as family members gather for a funeral,
they are reminded of the shortness of life.
Our time on God's earth is limited.
Shared tears and memories
strengthen the cords joining families together,
as our Creator's unending love and grace
surround and nurture us day by day.

MARY'S FAITH JOURNEY
LUKE 1:39-45
"FAMILY"

One of the most beloved persons in the Bible is Mary. Her humble origins and deep faith have attracted admirers for centuries. Mary seems open and approachable to the readers of her story in the New Testament. We cannot imagine her gossiping with the haughty and vain of her village.

One of the keys to understanding Mary is the importance of *family* in her life. In fact, it is an essential part of Mary's faith journey. Her bond with Elizabeth is highlighted in our reading in the Gospel of Luke.

The centrality of family in the life of Mary is consistent with the perspective of the Bible, both in the Old and New Testaments. The author of Psalm 107 puts it this way,

> He raises up the needy out of distress,
> and makes their families like flocks.
> The upright see it and are glad.
>   (Psalm 107:41-42)

God's goodness and love are revealed in the blessing of human families. In the Bible, there are biological families: the family of Abraham, the family of David, and the family of Joseph and Mary.

In another very important sense, the Bible lifts up the family of faith. All those who follow the living God are included in this spiritual family. This promise is especially dear to those who do are not part of a biological family.

Mary's faith journey, as recorded in our reading from the Gospel of Luke, shows us two important aspects of the role of family: *risk* and *reward*. We will look at both of them.

As Luke describes the value of family in Mary's journey, we note the *risk* involved. For Mary, there is the risk of being vulnerable. She journeys to spend time with Elizabeth who is identified in Luke 1:36 as her "relative" (New Revised Standard Version) or her "cousin" (King James Version). He writes,

> In those days Mary set out and went with haste to a Judean town in the hill country, where she entered the house of Zechariah and greeted Elizabeth (Luke 1:39-40).

In Mary's day, the "hill country" referred to the region south of Jerusalem. It is 64 miles from Nazareth in the north, Mary's home town, to Jerusalem in the south. It is estimated that such a journey would have taken Mary about 4-5 days.

Luke's Gospel is full of details about the daily activities of its main characters. In the first two chapters, he records that Mary made this long journey south to Jerusalem at least four times:

- Luke 1:39 – Mary visits Elizabeth.
- Luke 2:4 – Mary and Joseph go to Bethlehem for the birth of Jesus.
- Luke 2:22 – They go to Jerusalem for the sacrifice of purification.
- Luke 2:41 – They go to Jerusalem for the Passover.

It is clear that Joseph accompanies Mary on the journeys found in chapter two. Did she travel alone on the first journey? The Gospel of Luke is not 100% clear on this. It is after all a distance of over 60 miles. In order for Mary to be with her fellow family member, Elizabeth, she appears to have taken some *risk*.

Mary's experience shows the value of *family* as we make our faith journey. Families, however, are not perfect and expose us to *risk*. We are vulnerable to being disappointed or taken advantage of. We also suffer when members of our family suffer. How hard it must have been when Mary saw her son die on a cross (John 19:26).

There are two aspects to the role of family in our journey. Familial ties bring the *risk* of disappointment and sorrow. They also, however, bring the *reward* of bonding. This is expressed in the final lines of our poem:

> What's the glue that keeps a family connected? ...
> Shared tears and memories
> strengthen the cords joining families together,
> as our Creator's unending love and grace

surround and nurture us day by day.

Yes, families are not perfect. Yes, they can disappoint. There is, however, another side.

Mary shows us that these ties also bring the *reward* of bonding. Luke describes it with these words,

> She [Mary] entered the house of Zechariah and greeted Elizabeth. When Elizabeth heard Mary's greeting, the child leaped in her womb. And Elizabeth was filled with the Holy Spirit and exclaimed with a loud cry, "Blessed are you among women, and blessed is the fruit of your womb" (Luke 1:40-42).

What a joyful and affirming reunion between Mary and Elizabeth. They are of the same family, the same blood, the same DNA. For Mary, this warm welcome made the hardships of her long trek worth the effort.

Let us remember Mary as we continue on our own journey. May her experience of the love and support of *family* give us strength and hope. We are not alone.

REFLECTING ON MARY'S JOURNEY

1. Mary is one of the most beloved characters in the Bible. What makes her appealing to you?

2. Luke is not clear whether Mary traveled alone in order to visit Elizabeth. Do you think she did?

3. Many see Mary as a very meek person. Name one way in which Mary was strong?

4. Would Mary be comfortable with all the attention she gets? Why?

NEHEMIAH'S FAITH JOURNEY
"REPAIR"

So I came to Jerusalem and was there three days.
(Nehemiah 2:11)

NEHEMIAH 2:11-16

So I came to Jerusalem and was there for three days. Then I got up during the night, I and a few men with me; I told no one what my God had put into my heart to do for Jerusalem. The only animal I took was the animal I rode. I went out by night by the Valley Gate past the Dragon's Spring and to the Dung Gate, and I inspected the walls of Jerusalem that had been broken down and its gates that had been destroyed by fire. Then I went on to the Fountain Gate and to the King's Pool; but there was no place for the animal I was riding to continue. So I went up by way of the valley by night and inspected the wall. Then I turned back and entered by the Valley Gate, and so returned. The officials did not know where I had gone or what I was doing; I had not yet told the Jews, the priests, the nobles, the officials, and the rest that were to do the work.

"WORDS THAT HEAL"

Words often threaten and scare …
    they can cut and hurt
    can bloody and wound.

Will God speak a Word of healing?
    … maybe the world is beyond repair?
    … is restoration even possible?

The freed slaves gathered at Mount Sinai
    and listened for God's Word.
They heard the thunderous message
    and called it TORAH.
God's TORAH was their path to life.

Early followers of Jesus gathered in house-churches
    to worship the Word-Made-Flesh.
They called him LOGOS
    and built their lives around him.

God's TORAH, God's LOGOS bring life.
The message of the Bible
And the touch of the Risen Christ
    still heal the wounded
    and repair the broken.

NEHEMIAH'S FAITH JOURNEY
NEHEMIAH 2:11-16
"REPAIR"

About one mile from my house is a car repair shop owned by Charlie. I've known him for more than a decade and can testify that Charlie really, really knows cars. Just by listening to a running engine, he can tell you what needs to be repaired. It is amazing.

When members of my family purchased used cars, we took them to Charlie's shop so that he could check them out. Over the years, I've learned to rely on his judgment. If something is not working properly, Charlie can usually repair it in a couple of hours.

Over and over again in the Bible, we find this theme of *repair*. God's creation is broken, fallen and in need of repair or healing. These words of the prophet Isaiah illustrate this common theme,

> Your ancient ruins shall be rebuilt; you shall
> raise up the foundations of many generations;
> you shall be called the repairer of the breach,
> the restorer of streets to live in (Isaiah 58:12).

Isaiah is speaking to the people of Israel and encouraging them to take up the challenge of repairing the broken, sacked city of Jerusalem.

The faith journey of Nehemiah reflects this central biblical theme. He was one of the Jewish exiles living in the Persian capital of Susa. As the cupbearer to the king, Nehemiah held a prominent position. He learns that the walls of Jerusalem are in ruins and feels called by God to return to the "City of David" and organize the *repair* of the walls. The Persian King Artaxerxes grants Nehemiah permission and even gives him letters of safe passage. In fact, Nehemiah is appointed Governor of Judea.

This dramatic story is told in the first person by Governor Nehemiah. He journeys from Susa to Jerusalem to accomplish this great work of repairing the walls and gates. Listen to his account,

> So I came to Jerusalem and was there for three days. Then I got up during the night …. I inspected the walls of Jerusalem that had been broken down and its gates that had been destroyed by fire (Nehemiah 2:11-12, 13).

Nehemiah called himself God's "servant" (1:6) and was now seeing the enormity of the task in front of him.

In the Book of Nehemiah, the author gives us a first-person account of this massive repair project. He is clear about the amount of *preparation* needed. We have already seen from Nehemiah 2:13 that he "inspected" the broken-down walls of Jerusalem. The author carefully chooses his words here. Nehemiah did not simply "look" at what was left of the walls or "glance" at them. No. He carried out a careful inspection of them. Nehemiah sought to find out just what was involved in repairing them. How many new stones were needed? How many workers? How much time?

Nehemiah began the hard work of preparation. He knew that this was necessary before the project of repairing the walls could begin. It was needed in order for this project to have a chance of success.

When our faith journey gives us the opportunity to repair what is broken, do we take seriously the need to prepare? It's tempting to just dive into a situation without the hard work of considering what is needed.

The Book of Nehemiah tells an inspiring story. One man's faith journey brings restoration to both the walls of Jerusalem and to its inhabitants. Once Nehemiah has made a careful inspection of the broken walls, he then must challenge his fellow Jews to roll up their sleeves and get to work. This takes him into the necessity of *persuasion*. He says to the people,

> "You see the trouble we are in, how Jerusalem lies in ruins with its gates burned. Come, let us rebuild the wall of Jerusalem, so that we may no longer suffer disgrace" (Nehemiah 2:17).

Nehemiah's effort at persuasion goes on for several more verses. God blesses his words and the people respond with enthusiasm for this massive project.

This aspect of Nehemiah's journey was crucial. Could he

have repaired the walls by himself? Of course not. All of his preparations would have been useless unless the residents of Jerusalem rallied to his side. The rest of the book tells how together they accomplished the task.

And so it is with us. Each one of us is on a unique faith journey. In a real way, however, we are dependent on each other. God's work is bigger than any one of us can accomplish alone.

Nehemiah's journey shows God's desire to heal a broken, hurting creation. This is a fundamental theme in the Old and New Testaments. As the previous poem says,

> God's TORAH, God's LOGOS bring life.
> The message of the Bible
> And the touch of the Risen Christ
>   still heal the wounded
>   and repair the broken.

In the midst of difficult, divisive times, God loves his creation and desires its healing. As part of our faith journey, we hear God's call to help repair the broken.

REFLECTING ON NEHEMIAH'S JOURNEY

1. As Christians, do we spend more time condemning the world or trying to repair it?

2. Do you think that some residents of Jerusalem criticized Nehemiah for working with the Persians?

3. How does my faith journey affect the lives of others?

4. What aspect of Nehemiah's leadership style do you admire? Why?

LYDIA'S FAITH JOURNEY
"OPEN"

"If you have judged me to be faithful to the Lord,
come and stay at my home."
(Acts 16:15)

ACTS 16:11-15

We set sail from Troas and took a straight course to Samothrace, the following day to Neapolis, and from there to Philippi, which is a leading city of the district of Macedonia and a Roman colony. We remained in this city for some days. On the sabbath day we went outside the gate by the river, where we supposed there was a place of prayer; and we sat down and spoke to the women who had gathered there. A certain woman named Lydia, a worshiper of God, was listening to us; she was from the city of Thyatira and a dealer in purple cloth. The Lord opened her heart to listen eagerly to what was said by Paul. When she and her household were baptized, she urged us, saying, "If you have judged me to be faithful to the Lord, come and stay at my home." And she prevailed upon us.

"AN EASIER WAY"

Is there is an easier way?
Sometimes life has too many challenges
    and pressures.
An easier way would mean less effort
and fewer hours of labor
and we could stay in our comfort zone.

An easier way is not that hard to find.
The key word is, "CLOSED."
Life would be so much simpler
    if we were closed-minded,
    if we closed our eyes and ears
    and if our books remained closed.

But God calls spiritual pilgrims to OPEN .....
to open their hearts to the discouraged:
those who struggle with depression
those who fear the future
and those scarred by life's hardships.

God calls those on a faith journey to OPEN .....
to open their Bibles for divine guidance:
allowing the Spirit to breathe life into the words
following the path described in its pages
and living as citizens of the Kingdom.

God calls his followers to OPEN .....
to open doors that keep others out:
allowing neighbors into our homes
permitting strangers into our houses of worship
and welcoming the lost and despairing.

Is there an easier way?
Is there a BETTER way?

LYDIA'S FAITH JOURNEY
ACTS 16:11-15
"OPEN"

In grade school, I had to recite Luke 2:4 as part of our church's Christmas program. I memorized it in the King James Version:

> And Joseph also went up from Galilee, out
> of the city of Nazareth, into Judaea, unto
> the city of David, which is called Bethlehem.

I practiced and practiced this verse until I could recite it from memory to my mother. Years later, Luke 2:4 is still engrained in my memory. It is embedded in that classic King James language.

In this book, I'm using the New Revised Standard Version for my biblical quotes. This is how the NRSV translates Luke 2:4,

> Joseph also went from the town of Nazareth
> in Galilee to Judea, to the city of David called
> Bethlehem.

As you can see, there is a marked difference between these two translations. My eyes see one verse and my brain remembers another version of it. The beloved KJV was written 400 years ago. Am I open-minded enough to realize that modern translations are more accurate and easier to read?

This chapter will explore Lydia's faith journey. As we look closely at how the author of the Book of Acts describes her experience, the necessity of being *open* to God's unfolding plan becomes evident.

Our passage actually points to three separate journeys. Lydia is a busy person. We are told in verse 14 about her first journey:

> She was from the city of Thyatira and a dealer in purple cloth.

The city of Thyatira was about 250 miles southeast of Philippi. It was in Asia Minor, modern-day Turkey. Lydia had to sail across the Aegean Sea in order to arrive at the city of Philippi. We know that the city of Thyatira was famous for its purple dye and it seems that Lydia was one of the many who sold this purple cloth throughout the eastern Roman Empire.

From this information, we certainly know that Lydia was open to adventure and the risk of travel in the Roman world. Since we hear nothing about a husband, we assume that she was a single woman who had to make it on her own in the purple cloth industry.

Faith journeys are adventures. They take us out of our comfort zone. We meet new people. We must navigate new and unique situations. By traveling 250 miles across the Aegean Sea, Lydia proved her open attitude. Her faith journey would not be just routine.

Lydia's first journey from Thyatira to Philippi challenges our complacency. Are we content to remain in our comfort zone or are we *open* to whatever God may have in store for us?

We learn of Lydia's second journey in verse 13 where we are told that she meets Paul, "outside the gate by the river." Lydia had walked from her house in the city of Philippi to the Gangites River. She was part of a group of women who had gathered on the Sabbath at a place of prayer by this river.

As a "worshiper of God," Lydia was most likely a Gentile who was attracted to the Jewish teaching about the "one true God." By being at this place of prayer outside of the city, Lydia showed that she was open to God speaking to her and acting in her life.

This second journey of Lydia was much shorter than her first one. Her walk to the meeting place by the Gangites River, however, was just as significant. By meeting Paul, Lydia had the opportunity to receive a message that would transform her life. Lydia's openness is a model for us. We need to seek out places, occasions, or persons that can be avenues of God's message for us.

There is a third faith journey. Lydia believes Paul's message and is baptized. She then says,

> "If you have judged me to be faithful to the Lord, come and stay at my home" (v. 15).

Paul accepts her invitation. There is now a journey to her house in Philippi and the giving of hospitality to Paul. This person who until recently had been an unknown stranger to Lydia, was now her special guest.

What a remarkable step of faith for Lydia. The previous poem captures the dynamics of her third journey with these words,

> God calls his followers to OPEN ….
> to open doors that keep others out:
> > allowing neighbors into our homes
> > permitting strangers in our houses of worship
> > and welcoming the lost and despairing.

What a remarkable person. Lydia's openness to Paul and his message impresses us even today. We can only imagine the conversations that took place in her house. Lydia's life would be changed by this experience.

A little boy worked hard to memorize Luke 2:4 and the words of that verse were itched in his mind. In later years, God's grace would open him to the beauty and clarity of newer translations. May each one of us experience that same grace on our faith journey.

REFLECTING ON LYDIA'S JOURNEY

1. While each of Lydia's three faith journeys is impressive, which one is your favorite? Why?

2. Are you as open as Lydia?

3. Have you met someone like Lydia?

4. How did God prepare Lydia for her encounter with Paul by the River Gangites?

PETER'S FAITH JOURNEY
"HOPE"

When they had gone ashore, they saw a charcoal fire there, with fish on it, and bread (John 21:9).

JOHN 21:9-19

When they had gone ashore, they saw a charcoal fire there, with fish on it, and bread. Jesus said to them, "Bring some of the fish that you have just caught." So Simon Peter went aboard and hauled the net ashore, full of large fish, a hundred fifty-three of them; and though there were so many, the net was not torn. Jesus said to them, "Come and have breakfast." Now none of the disciples dared to ask him, "Who are you?" because they knew it was the Lord. Jesus came and took the bread and gave it to them, and did the same with the fish. This was now the third time that Jesus appeared to the disciples after he was raised from the dead.

When they had finished breakfast, Jesus said to Simon Peter, "Simon son of John, do you love me more than these?" He said to him, "Yes, Lord; you know that I love you." Jesus said to him, "Feed my lambs." A second time he said to him, "Simon son of John, do you love me?" He said to him, "Yes, Lord; you know that I love you." Jesus said to him, "Tend my sheep." He said to him the third time, "Simon son of John, do you love me?" Peter felt hurt because he said to him the third time, "Do you love me?" And he said to him, "Lord, you know everything; you know that I love you." Jesus said to him, "Feed my sheep." Very truly, I tell you, when you were younger, you used to fasten your own belt and to go wherever you wished. But when you grow old, you will stretch out your hands, and someone else will fasten a belt around you and take you where you do not wish to go." (He said this to indicate the kind of death by which he would glorify God.) After this he said to him, "Follow me."

"HOPE COMES"

Like a cool breeze on a hot day,
Hope comes.
It comes …..
to those who weep:
      drying their tears
      and hugging their shaking frame.

Like fresh water in the desert,
Hope comes.
It comes …..
to those who stumble:
      gently lifting them up
      and steadying their uncertain steps.

Like a sunrise piercing the darkness,
Hope comes.
It comes …..
to those who are lost:
      comforting their fears
      and leading them to safety.

Like flowers coming to life in the spring,
Hope comes.
It comes …..
to those who seek the truth:
      opening the Book for them
      and introducing the Word-Made-Flesh.

PETER'S FAITH JOURNEY
JOHN 21:9-19
"HOPE"

I had the opportunity to serve as a missionary at the Colegio Americano in Caracas, Venezuela. I was the chaplain of the school and worked with a local task force to build a chapel and plant a new church on campus. In the midst of all of Venezuela's troubles, we decided to name the new congregation, *Iglesia Presbiteriana la Esperanza* ("Hope Presbyterian Church").

The people of that suffering country desperately needed a message of *hope*. Sensing this need, the new church chose Romans 15:13 as its theme verse. It is here that Paul refers to God in Greek as, *theos tēs elpidos* ("the God of hope"). With these words, the apostle reveals an essential aspect of the divine character. The living God of the Old and New Testaments is a Giver-of-Hope.

In Peter's faith journey, we see the truth of this verse and its life-changing power. Peter makes a journey from the city of Jerusalem north to the Sea of Galilee, about seventy miles. It is a journey that changes his life.

Peter's journey begins with his denial of Jesus in Jerusalem. This is described in the Gospel of John, chapter 18. Jesus has been arrested and is being questioned in the court of the high priest. Peter is present in the waiting crowd and three different persons accuse him of being a follower of the arrested teacher from Galilee. Peter denies Jesus three times:

- v. 17 [a woman says] "You are not also one of this man's disciples, are you?"
  [Peter replies] "I am not."
- v. 25 [They asked] "You are not also one of his disciples, are you?"
  [Peter says] "I am not."
- v. 26 [a slave asks] "Did I not see you in the garden with him?"
  [v. 27] "Again Peter denied it."

The other three Gospel writers tell us that Peter realized the error of his denials and was devastated. He left the courtyard of the high priest and wept bitterly. We can only imagine what the other disciples thought of him.

Where was Peter to turn? How could he go on living? How awkward it must have been for him after the resurrection of Jesus. His fellow disciples knew that he had denied their Lord three times in the courtyard of the high priest.

Perhaps the greatest barrier to taking a faith journey is the feeling of despair or hopelessness. We can easily fall into such a sad state of mind, state of emotion when we encounter difficult moments in life. How can we take the first steps of the journey?

Peter had to walk from the *despair* of his denial in

Jerusalem to the *hope* of a new encounter with the Risen Christ at the Sea of Galilee. We leave the bitter disappointment of John chapter 18 and now look at what happens to Peter in chapter 21.

We remember the description of God that we found in Romans 15:13: "the God of hope." Peter's only chance is to put his trust in this living God who has revealed himself in the Bible and in Jesus. As we read in the poem,

> Like flowers coming to life in the spring,
> Hope comes.
> It comes ....
> to those who seek the truth:
> > opening the Book for them
> > and introducing the Word-Made-Flesh.

Peter's encounter with Jesus will heal his *despair* and fill him with *hope*.

Just as John records Peter's three denials in chapter 18, he now records his three confessions of faith in chapter 21. This parallel structure is no coincidence. The author of the Fourth Gospel is making sure that the reader does not miss the connection between these events. What was broken, Jesus now heals. Peter's journey from Jerusalem to the Sea of Galilee was not in vain.

In front of the other disciples, Jesus asks Peter three times if he loves him. Each time, Peter publicly declares his love for his Master. John records the three replies:

- v. 15 "Yes, Lord; you know that I love you."
- v. 16 "Yes, Lord; you know that I love you."
- v. 17 "Lord, you know everything; you know that I love you."

Peter's hope is rekindled. His place among the disciples is restored. When we begin to read the Book of Acts, we see him functioning as a key leader in the early church.

In the New Testament, there are two letters that tradition has ascribed to Peter. In First Peter 1:3, we get a sense of his profound, life-changing experience of hope:

> Blessed be the God and Father of our Lord Jesus Christ! By his great mercy he has given us a new birth into a living hope (*elpida zōsan*) through the resurrection of Jesus Christ from the dead.

Years after his encounter with the Risen Lord on the shore of the Sea of Galilee, Peter could still celebrate a faith journey filled with hope.

REFLECTING ON PETER'S JOURNEY

1. Was Peter qualified to be one of the key leaders of the early church?

2. What was Peter thinking as he journeyed from Jerusalem to the Sea of Galilee?

3. Does it make a difference in our faith journey if we encounter the Almighty as the "God of hope"?

4. Is Peter's experience unique?

PART TWO
LITURGIES AND POEMS

"A NEW SONG"

"O sing to the Lord a new song,
for he has done marvelous things!"
Lord, I hear your words of instruction.
Are you waiting for me to sing a new song?
Listening for music that is alive and real?

But Lord, I'm comfortable with my old song.
I've whistled and sung the same notes for years.
I know that familiar tune backwards and forwards.
It's my song and it's done my way.

"O sing to the Lord a new song,
for he has done marvelous things!"
The songs of God's Kingdom touch us.
They melt hardened hearts and fill us with joy.
Our souls respond with praise,
with awe, and with gratitude.

O Lord, let my song give way to your song.

                (from Psalm 98:1)

"AND HIS FACE SHONE"

Peter, James, and John obey their Master
And the three friends begin their ascent.
They closely follow the Rabbi.
With a sense of purpose, Jesus walks up the path.
His steps are sure and firm.
The steepness of the trail does not bother him.

Will something happen today?
There is no crowd to teach.
There are no blind beggars to heal.
There is no raging sea to calm.
There are no scribes and Pharisees to debate.
There is no child to bless.

What is waiting at the summit?
What does Jesus have planned?

"And his face shone like the sun … "
This is no ordinary day.
The very glory of God is blazing forth
And the glowing majesty of the Divine is present.
Peter, James, and John are filled with awe.

"And his face shone like the sun … "
Moses and Elijah speak with the promised Messiah
And a voice comes from the cloud.
No. This is no ordinary day.
The divine glory of the very Son of God
Shines forth and nearly blinds them.

Like these disciples
We, too, need to follow Jesus as he leads.
We, too, need to walk along his path.
We, too, need to open our lives
To his majestic, divine presence.
"And his face shone like the sun ... "

(from Matthew 17:1-8)

"BEING A FATHER"

Being a father is not easy ... you must
>be wise and give good advice
>be strong and protect the weak
>be confident and encourage the timid
>be loving and embrace the downhearted.

Being a father is not easy ... just ask ABRAHAM
>God tells him to sacrifice Isaac, his promised son
>he binds Isaac and raises the knife
>in the last moment God provides a ram
>Abraham can breathe again.

Being a father is not easy ... just ask JACOB
>he gives Joseph a coat of many colors
>his other sons plot against "the favored one"
>the family suffers strife and is divided
>reconciliation and reunion will take years.

Being a father is not easy ... just ask JESSE
>one of his eight sons will become king
>David, the youngest, is chosen and anointed
>Jesse must witness David's triumphs and failures
>he both rejoices and weeps over his son.

Abraham, Jacob, and Jesse show us the truth ...
>being a father is not easy.

In the midst of our struggle with expectations and doubts,
>we hear the promise given in God's Word,
>>"I can do all things
>>>through him who strengthens me."

(from Philippians 4:13)

"EASTER LIGHT"

It's easy to stumble in the dark.
When darkness reigns over the earth
There is no hope, no sunshine, no joy.
When darkness reigns
Wars multiply, hunger ravages, diseases kill.

The women come to the tomb in darkness
Hoping to anoint the body of their crucified Lord.
Sinister forces had claimed a victim.
They had crucified the Giver of Light.
They had killed the Author of Hope.

But … John boldly proclaims that
The Light shines in the darkness
And the darkness has not overcome it.
The women arrive at an Empty Tomb
And they are the first to hear
The Good News of the Resurrection.

(from John 1:1-5)

"FIRST PALM SUNDAY"

All the city is stirred …
    excitement is building,
    there is expectation in the air,
    young and old are rushing to see,
    someone is coming.

"Hosanna to the Son of David!"
    Who is that?
    Is it Mary's first-born son?
    Is it the rabbi from Nazareth in Galilee?
    Is it the healer of the lame and the blind?

"Blessed is he who comes in the name of the Lord!"
    We need someone to come …
    there must be a Deliverer who is able …
    there must be a Savior who can …
    there must be a Rescuer who is strong enough …

"Hosanna in the highest!"
    Save us, O God!
    For we cannot save ourselves.
    We try and we try and we try.
    We know our limits and our frailties.

All the city is stirred …
    He enters Jerusalem:
    those who Hope … shout with joy
    those who Doubt … watch in silence
    those who Hate … put their plot in motion.

"Hosanna in the highest!"
    Save us, O God!
    For we cannot save ourselves.

                (from Matthew 21:1-10)

"FOLLOW ME"

The rabbi from Nazareth is in our synagogue today.
I came early to sit near the front.
Jesus will amaze us with his knowledge of Torah.
He knows more than the teachers in Jerusalem.
I wait for his instructions ….
He just says, "Follow me."

The great story-teller has packed our little synagogue.
His parables are so entertaining.
There is the Lost Sheep, the Good Samaritan,
And the Wise and Foolish Builders.
I am eager to another story ….
He just says, "Follow me."

The healer from Galilee has attracted a crowd.
Would he perform wonders on this Sabbath?
Would the lame walk or the blind see?
We would be eyewitnesses of his great deeds.
While I wait to be astonished ….
He just says, "Follow me."

Jesus, don't miss this opportunity.
You have such a big crowd today.
Amaze us with your ….
     understanding of Torah
     witty parables
     mighty healings
He stands to leave and says,
     "Follow me."
What do I do now?

(from John 1:43)

"GIFTS"

What gifts do I want?
Every day my senses are overwhelmed.

My ears hear of all the things I don't have ...
    a new gadget now on sale
    a device that will save me time
    a service available in my town.
My eyes see what will make me happy ...
    the latest fashion in the stores
    the fastest car now on the lot
    the newest show on cable.

Am I deaf? Am I blind?
Do I hear or see gifts already received?
    soothing words spoken by a friend
    the sound of a special hymn
    laughter of those I love
    a radiant sunset that ends the day
    the sight of my favorite verse
    a smiling face that shares God's love.

"IN THE NAME OF THE LORD"

While waving palms, the crowd shouts ....
    "Hosanna!
    Blessed is the one who comes in the name of the Lord!"
The man riding on a donkey nods his head;
he smiles at those caught up in the excitement.

Others have also entered Jerusalem with great anticipation.
Pharisees came into the city ....
    "in the name of the Torah."
They wanted to create a holy city;
a city based on their narrow interpretation of the Law.

Merchants entered Jerusalem from all over the Middle East.
Eager for trade and profit, they came ....
    "in the name of the shekel."
They dreamed of gold and silver as
they set up tables in the temple courtyard.

Romans marched into Jerusalem as proud conquerors.
These battle-hardened veterans came ....
    "in the name of Caesar."
They trusted in their swords and tactics;
confident that brute force would break the will of the Jews.

How different is the entrance of Jesus.
His dream for Jerusalem is not based on
    legalism or profit or violence.
He comes to proclaim the Kingdom of God.
And the crowd waves palms and shouts ....
    "Hosanna!
    Blessed is the one who comes in the name of the Lord!"

                    (from John 12:12-19)

"LIVING AND REVEALING GOD"

We human beings can be so curious.
What's over the next hill?
>   maybe a meadow, forest or lake

What's at the bottom of the ocean?
>   perhaps some new and strange species

What's in the deep reaches of space?
>   possibly an undiscovered sun and earth

And the Creator and Sustainer of all this ...
Is it possible to meet and know such a Being?
What if this Being is a living and revealing God?
And this God has implanted our sense of curiosity?

The living God is revealed
as Father ...
>   calling us his very own sons and daughters
>   inviting us into his worldwide family.

as Son ...
>   sharing our humanity and bearing our sin
>   rising from the grave and giving us eternal life.

as Holy Spirit ...
>   giving us gifts to build up the community of faith
>   producing fruit to bring hope and healing to the world.

Is it possible to meet and know God?
What if God is a living and revealing God?
Today we affirm the Bible's reply of "Yes."
Brothers and sisters, this is Good News.

"MAKE ME WISE"

Lord, some days I feel foolish.
I can't seem to understand what's happening.
Change is so fast, so rapid, so unsettling.
It feels like I'm walking on shaky, unstable ground.

Grant me your wisdom, O Lord.
May I discern your path.
When the world judges those who are different
…. let me value all of your creatures.

May the light of your wisdom shine on me, O Lord.
Let me never be satisfied walking in darkness.
As the world embraces violence as a solution
…. may I follow the Prince of Peace.

Lord, may I hear the voice of your wisdom.
The shouts of the foolish seem so urgent and loud.
While the world so quickly believes in lies
…. strengthen my commitment to uncover the truth.

O God, when I feel foolish
…. fill me with your wisdom.
When I get confused
…. straighten out my priorities.
Lord, when I stand at a fork in the road
…. grant me discernment to make a wise choice.

"THAT STONE'S TOO BIG"

Walking to the tomb early in the morning ….
    thinking: That stone's too big.
    worrying: What will we do?
    praying: O God help us!

The women carry spices to anoint
    the body of their fallen Lord.
It's the first day of the week.
It's dawn and they are ….
    thinking: That stone's too big.
    worrying: What will we do?
    praying: O God help us!

The earth begins to rumble,
There's a shaking of the ground.
Something strange is happening and they are ….
    thinking: That stone's too big.
    worrying: What will we do?
    praying: O God help us!

An angel appears,
a dazzling whiteness shines forth ….
    The stone is rolled away.
    The tomb is empty.
    The Lord is Risen indeed!

As we journey, we wrestle with so many burdens.
    Life batters us.
    Life tests our faith.

And we walk ….
    thinking: That stone's too big.
    worrying: What will we do?
    praying: O God help us!

    (from Mark 16:1-8)

"THE SEVENTH MONTH"

I love the seventh month of the year.
If I had my way,
I'd just skip January through June.
Give me good-old July …
I love these thirty-one special days.

What other month starts off with fireworks?
All over this land,
towns and villages come together
on one night to watch
a show of shooting, exploding stars.

July is for trips to the beach.
It's in the middle of summer …
a time for sunscreen, an umbrella, and a cooler.
The water temp is ideal,
bring a couple of beach chairs.

In the middle of such a festive month
these words fit right in:
"Joy to the World. The Lord is come.
Let earth receive her King.
Let every heart prepare him room."

I love the seventh month of the year.
If I had my way,
I'd just skip January through June.
Give me good-old July …
I love these thirty-one special days.

(This was written for a *Christmas in July* service.)

"THE WORLD NEEDS EASTER"

The world is stuck in Good Friday.
When our Lord was crucified ...
    there was violence, brokenness, injustice.
In places far and wide today ...
    we see violence, brokenness, injustice.
We need Easter morning!

Evil appeared victorious on that first Good Friday.
The haters, mockers, and killers seemed to win.
While soldiers watched over the crowd,
    the Prince of Peace was put to death on a cross.
The Roman world needed Easter morning.

The world is stuck in Good Friday when ...
    little children go hungry,
    innocent people are killed,
    hatred replaces love,
    division destroys unity.
We need Easter morning!

Are you stuck in Good Friday?
    Have you lost hope?
    Do you despair over a broken world?
    Are you overwhelmed by the cries of the hurting?
    Do you feel helpless and afraid?
You need Easter morning!

"THIS EASTER MORNING"

What does the world need this Easter morning?
What would
    fill the void,
    bridge the gap,
    bring a smile?

Let's share a cute little rabbit.
This would turn frowns into smiles,
the cold would find warmth,
children could chase it around the yard.

How about baskets of painted eggs?
What a joy there would be in decorating them,
we could hide them,
some could be made of chocolate.

What about a brand-new bonnet?
It could match a new outfit,
imagine the fun of showing it off,
and others will be so jealous.

Would the Risen Lord have a following?
The broken could be mended,
the despairing receive hope,
and the lonely embraced by Love.

It's worth a try.

"THRONES AND CHAIRS"

Some days I dream of sitting on a throne ….
    the world will be at my feet
    people will hang on my every word
    I will be the envy of all who see me.

Most days I find myself sitting in a chair ….
    an ordinary, plain, common, average-looking one
    nothing fancy, nothing extravagant
    I'm not sure that I like this.

Sometimes on Sunday, I sit in a pew ….
    some of the hymns I don't know
    I can't find Obadiah or Nahum in the Bible
    at least people smile at me.

I would really like to sit on a grassy hill ….
    the sun would feel warm and the breeze cool
    what a place to make sense of life
    I hear that Jesus used to sit there.

"WAITING FATHER"

The sun rises and signals the beginning of a new day.
The owner of the farm begins to walk around ...
    busy hours of work lie ahead
    there are workers to be supervised
    crops that must be tended.
Will he again pause and look to the horizon?
Yes, there he goes again.
Doesn't he know that his son will not come back.
Long ago he left for a far country.

The noonday sun beats down without mercy.
Work must pause as everyone seeks shade and water.
Again, the owner looks to the horizon ...
    maybe today his prayers will be answered
    his heart longs for a miracle.
Is his missing son even alive?
He tries not to dwell on this thought.

The sun sets on a long day of work and toil.
Much has been accomplished
    and much remains to be done tomorrow.
The owner is tired and yet he begins to run.
The father recognizes a walking figure on the horizon ...
    he knows the tilt of the head
    and the special gait.
Countless prayers have been answered.
Kill the fatted calf and make merry!

        (from Luke 15:11-24)

"WHAT I HAVE"

I walk through a crowded marketplace.
There are too many people
    too many distractions
    too much noise.

Remember ... I have to
    clutch my purse
    put my wallet in a front pocket
    avoid crowded places.

I've got to protect what I have
    what is mine.
I won't take what is yours
Let me keep the little I have.

Yet, God keeps whispering to me ...
    it is unrelenting
    it is challenging.
Do my possessions own me?
Is the fear of losing things
    shrinking my soul
    robbing me of joy?

O Lord, mold me according to your will
    calm my fears
    sooth my anxious spirit.
Teach me your ways.
Free me from things
And bless me with the joy of sharing.

"WHEN IS CHRISTMAS?"

When is Christmas?
Christmas is when a child is too excited to sleep
Dawn never seems to come
And the presents remain unopened.

When is Christmas?
It's when family and friends gather
A festive meal is shared, ties are strengthened
We celebrate our common blood and heritage.

When is Christmas?
Maybe when carolers lift up their voices
Songs of joy fill the night air
And fresh apple cider warms us up.

But, when is Christmas, really?
Christmas is when Jesus comes
When he replaces our sorrow with joy
When he brings healing to a broken world.

"WHERE DO WE LOOK?"

Jerusalem is crowded with pilgrims.
Happens every year at Passover.
The air is filled with strange-sounding words of
    Greeks, Egyptians, Persians,
    Romans, Parthians, and Medes.

Philip is stopped by certain Greeks.
"We wish to see Jesus."
    Are these Greeks part of the plot to arrest him?
    Are they secret admirers of Jesus?
Who are they?

"We wish to see Jesus. Where do we look?"
These Greeks have many options.
Maybe Jesus is with the Pharisees?
    They could see Jesus discussing the Law of Moses,
    Using the law to oppress and condemn others.

Should they look for Jesus at the Roman barracks?
The legions of Rome really hold the power.
Jesus could befriend the commanders and centurions.
    In case of violence, he would be on the winning
        side.
    Siding with the Romans would be a smart move.

Where are the rich? Can Jesus be seen with them?
Their houses are filled with luxuries.
    The hard work is done by slaves
    And they eat only the finest food.
    Jesus would enjoy this.

The Greeks tell Philip, "We wish to see Jesus."
Philip knows where to look.
> Jesus can be found feeding the hungry.
> He is giving sight to the blind.
> Jesus is embracing the outcasts and the rejected.

(from John 12:20-26)

"WHERE?"

On a mountain in Israel, Jesus' divine glory was revealed.
Peter, James, and John saw the brightness of his majesty.
They were in awe of this life-changing event.
Where does Jesus shine today?

Does Jesus shine where war rages?
Where ….
>mothers clutch tightly to their children
>families run for shelter to escape bombs
>doctors try to save the wounded.

Does Jesus shine where people are hungry?
Where ….
>little money means precious little food
>growth is stunted
>hunger pangs will not go away.

Does Jesus shine where people are divided?
Where ….
>the "common good" is not valued
>the poor are not seen
>races are suspicious and afraid.

Where does Jesus shine today?
Wherever ….
>we become one of the peacemakers
>we embrace all of God's children
>we lift up the values of his Kingdom.

(from Luke 9:28-36)

"WORD"

The writers of Scripture
    constantly mention the "Word."
What is this Word? ….. Who is the Word?

Isaiah says that the Word will accomplish its purpose.
    It is like the rain that brings life;
        dormant seeds will sprout and grow.
This Word strengthens the weak,
    comforts the afflicted,
        heals the broken-hearted.

Jeremiah proclaims the Word
    to all of the cities of Judah
    and in the streets of Jerusalem.
God speaks his Word to all peoples.
This Word is not limited to one nation,
    one people or one time.
Its message crosses the barriers of language,
    custom, and culture.

John writes that this Word became flesh
    and dwelt among us,
        full of grace and truth.
Jesus reveals the glory of his heavenly Father
His teachings guide us even today
And he walks beside us on our journey of faith.

(from Isaiah 55:10-11, Jeremiah 11:6, John 1:14)

ABOUT THE AUTHOR

Robert Wierenga's life is a series of journeys. He grew up in western Michigan where he pastored his first church, Trinity Reformed Church of Grand Rapids. His family then moved to San José, Costa Rica for one year of Spanish language study. He spent most of the 1990s working as a mission partner with the  Presbyterian Church of Venezuela. His family moved to Caracas where Robert served as chaplain of the *Colegio Americano* and pastor of a new church. The Wierengas then journeyed to Tampa Bay, Florida where Robert served for twelve years as pastor of the Lake Seminole Presbyterian Church. He is now the founder/director of Wierenga Consulting, LLC.

Robert is married to Helen Mulder Wierenga and has three grown sons. He has a bachelor's degree from Grand Valley State University, a master's degree from Western Theological Seminary, and a Doctor of Ministry degree from Princeton Theological Seminary. Robert was also involved in campus ministry at the University of Michigan.

In both Grand Rapids and Tampa Bay, Robert was an active member of the local Rotary Club. He served as president of the West Grand Rapids Rotary Club.

TWO OTHER BOOKS AVAILABLE

 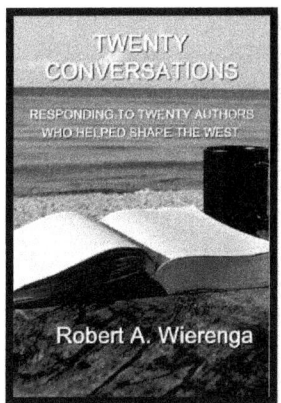

The print editions of my two previous books are available through Wierenga Consulting, LLC. *Twenty Conversations* is also available as an eBook on Amazon.

Leadership Styles Inventory is a practical manual based on my research on four basic leadership styles. It can be helpful individually or in a group setting.

Twenty Conversations examines selections from key authors, playwrights, and poets whose works have shaped Western culture.

NOTES

www.ingramcontent.com/pod-product-compliance
Lightning Source LLC
Chambersburg PA
CBHW071134090426
42736CB00012B/2124